REALISTIC PUMPKIN CARVING

24 SCARY, SPOOKY, AND SPINE-CHILLING DESIGNS

LUNDY CUPP

FOX CHAPEL
PUBLISHING

A *Woodcarving Illustrated* Book
www.WoodCarvingIllustrated.com

DEDICATION

For my son Wyatt, who renewed the sense of wonder that my dad instilled in me; who reintroduced the imagination that often escapes us when we grow older; who, from the day he was born, brought an intensity of love that I didn't even know existed.

Wyatt, travel through this life doing the things that make your heart soar. Never stop wondering. Never stop imagining. Never stop laughing and making others laugh. Take risks even when you're afraid. Most of all, be you. You are the best thing that ever happened to me. I sure do love you, son. More than anything in the whole wide world.

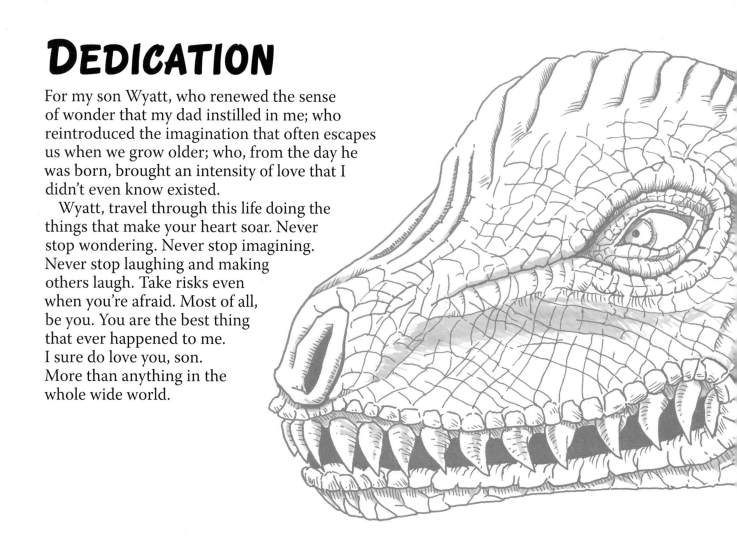

Realistic Pumpkin Carving is an original work first published in 2016 by Fox Chapel Publishing, Inc. Portions of this book were originally published in *Woodcarving Illustrated* magazine. The projects and patterns contained herein are copyrighted by the author. Readers may make copies of these patterns for personal use. The patterns themselves, however, are not to be duplicated for resale or distribution under any circumstances. Any such copying is a violation of copyright law.

ISBN 978-1-56523-894-7

To learn more about the other great books from Fox Chapel Publishing, or to find a retailer near you, call toll-free 800-457-9112 or visit us at *www.FoxChapelPublishing.com*.

Note to Authors: We are always looking for talented authors to write new books. Please send a brief letter describing your idea to Acquisition Editor, 1970 Broad Street, East Petersburg, PA 17520.

Printed in Singapore
First printing

ABOUT THE AUTHOR

Lundy Cupp is a carver and sculptor residing in the small, picturesque town of Kingston Springs, located outside of Nashville, Tenn. He accidentally discovered carving in 2005. He did not grow up carving or drawing, and it surprised him as much as anyone else that he had an undiscovered artistic talent. With this talent came passion, and he is certain he will be carving for the rest of his life.

Lundy has always had an entrepreneurial spirit and has taken risks to do things that interest him. As a child, he learned how to play the drums and became a professional musician at a young age. After many years in the music business, he jumped into a completely different profession—private investigation. He worked in the private sector with a couple of investigation companies, had a short stint as a surety recovery agent (which is a fancy name for bounty hunter), and then decided to start his own company, which became very successful in exposing criminal fraud. Lundy and his staff specialized in surveillance, locating missing persons, and undercover investigations for corporations. They also assisted various district attorney offices as expert witnesses.

After many years of owning and running his investigation company, practically living on airplanes and in cars, Lundy felt the stress taking its toll. This is when, one evening in his home in Tennessee, he picked up a piece of wood from his fire pit, brought it inside, and proceeded to flabbergast himself by carving it into a beautiful, flame-shaped vase. He found such joy in carving that he tried carving a face into another piece of wood. That's where and how it all began.

Now, art is Lundy's primary focus. He is completely self-taught and embraces trial and error as an important part of his process, no matter what he works with. Lundy carves and sculpts pretty much any material that can be cut, molded, or shaped, including wood, clay,

PHOTO BY RICK MALKIN

stone, pumpkins, sweet potatoes, various other fruits and vegetables, golf balls, and books. His inspiration comes from the living world that surrounds him; however, he enjoys working with the human face and form the most because he finds that the body and face can express an endless amount of emotion.

Lundy has been featured on two PBS television shows (*Tennessee Crossroads* and *Tennessee's Wildside*), local newscasts, *Nashville Arts Magazine*, and multiple blogs, including one by the editor of *Fine Books and Collections*. He is also a proud contributor to the magazine *Woodcarving Illustrated*, which has featured his pumpkin and wood carvings. He has carved pumpkins at The Cheekwood Botanical Garden and Museum of Art in Nashville, Tenn., as well as at parties for international movie stars, musicians, and sports figures.

To see more of Lundy's work, visit his website at www.LundyCupp.com.

CONTENTS

PROJECTS

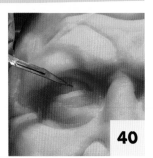

TECHNIQUES

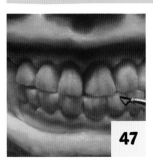

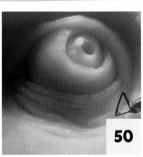

PATTERNS

INTRODUCTION

I ventured into the world of pumpkin carving in October 2009. My pumpkins were crude, but certainly different from traditional jack-o'-lanterns. When the kids in the neighborhood got wind that "Mr. Lundy" was carving pumpkins, I got tiny knocks on my door from curious, soon-to-be Halloween ghouls. I showed them the uncarved side of the pumpkin first and then theatrically turned the pumpkin around to show the carving. I knew I was on the right track because, more often than not, I was treated to a spectacular range of emotions on their little faces—from fascination to actual fear. It was great! They loved it, and so did I.

A few years later, I'm showing my pumpkin carvings to more than just the neighborhood kids. These pumpkin carvings have put me on the map as a carver and a sculptor, and I am so grateful.

Part of the major draw of pumpkin carving may be its ephemeral nature. This art form comes around only one month out of the year and, on top of that, the materials don't last very long. People often ask if it bothers me that my creations will soon rot, and my answer is always no. I take photos of all of my pumpkin carvings, and I know there will always be more. Plus, I learn from every one I carve.

Dig in fearlessly—but don't stop at just pumpkins. There are endless amounts of fruits, vegetables, and roots available year-round to carve.

I've done a lot of experimenting in the last couple of years, so I wanted to include carvings of different fruits and vegetables in this book. The Getting Started section includes information on prepping, carving, and preserving pumpkins, gourds, squashes, and sweet potatoes. The gallery showcases some of my carved creations, which range from friendly to creepy. The beginner step-by-step project shows you how to carve an Autumn Wings gourd, and the advanced step-by-step project focuses on carving a pumpkin. The Techniques section deep-dives into carving teeth and eyes. With the Techniques section and step-by-step projects, you'll be more than ready to take on the carvings in the Patterns section.

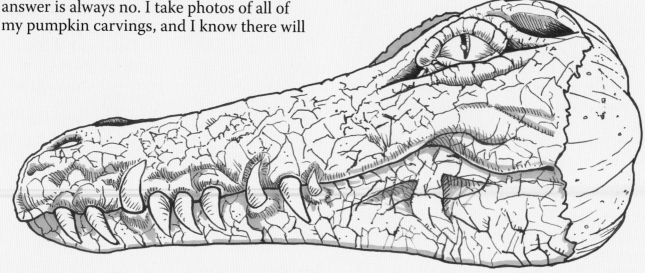

ARTIST'S STATEMENT

I'd like to share a short self-discovery story that changed my life as an artist. I have a feeling this applies to many artists at some point. After carving for two or three years, I developed a mental block. My skill level was progressing, but every time I got to a certain point in a carving, I would put it off and find an excuse to start another piece. Being an analytical guy, I started exploring why. I discovered that my carvings intimidated me when I thought that the piece looked good and I didn't want to screw it up. But in my mind and my heart, I knew it wasn't finished.

I had several unfinished pieces lying around (like the Green Man pictured), but was afraid to touch them. Once I realized this, I tried an experiment. I got a new piece of wood and promised myself that no one except me would ever see this piece. I decided to carve with no fear and be aggressive. I dug in and really went for it. It was an epiphany, a breakthrough! The freedom I felt was incredible, and I instantly became a better and faster carver. I never rush through my work—I enjoy the slow pace of my process. But when I say "faster," I mean I can complete the project to my satisfaction, and then I have the joy of starting a new one.

Fear can be a powerful thing that holds people back from exploring their creativity. You have already pushed at least some of that aside just by purchasing this book. You are attempting to learn and push yourself into new areas. I often hear, "I could never do that" and, "I have no creative ability." Unless you've tried, giving it a good shot with some dedication and time, how do you really know?

Don't start with the most complicated project and expect it to be great. Take carving, for instance. Start with something reasonable, like a pumpkin or a sweet potato or an apple—something that doesn't require expensive tools and weeks to complete. Pick up a pencil and doodle. Draw something that is out of your comfort zone, and don't judge yourself too harshly. No one has to see it but you. This simple task may open a window to a world you didn't even know existed within you.

I believe the desire to create art of some form is in all of us. But one usually doesn't just decide to be an artist. It often starts as a hobby, and we do it for the sheer joy of creating. Only when others outside my immediate circle of friends and family began recognizing my work did I even realize that I had real talent and skill. That was the catalyst to dedicate myself to learn more and develop my skills, confidence, and creative path.

I look at the world differently than I did before I discovered my abilities as an artist. I see the beauty in both the simple and the complex. The learning and discovery process never ends. Ever. That's what makes this whole art thing work, what makes it so much fun and addicting. It's the magic that drives the wonders of art.

Lundy

Lundy Cupp

This unfinished Green Man hangs in my photo studio as a reminder not to let fear hold me back

GALLERY

Look into My Eyes

Clifton Cushaw

Spud Nick

Bassingbourne

Trouble (Jarrahdale Pumpkin)

Ichabod >

Madden

Pumpkin Princess

Subdude

Are You Serious

I Wanted to Be a Pie

Buster

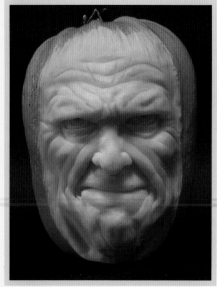

Argus

Centenarian Selma

Is That a Scalpel?

Uncle Joe >

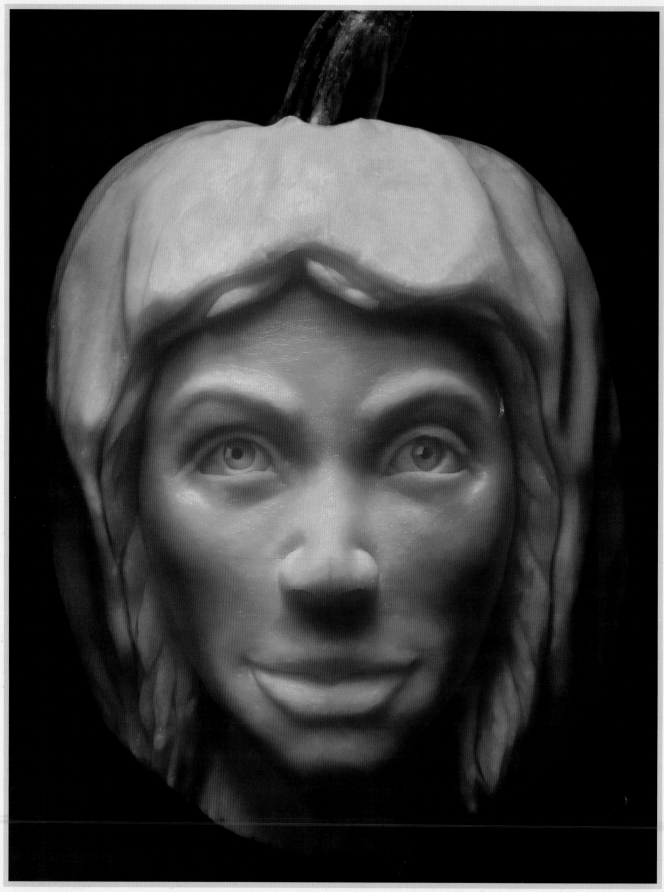

Girl in Hood

Butternut Bob
(Butternut Squash)

Harland

Disgusted

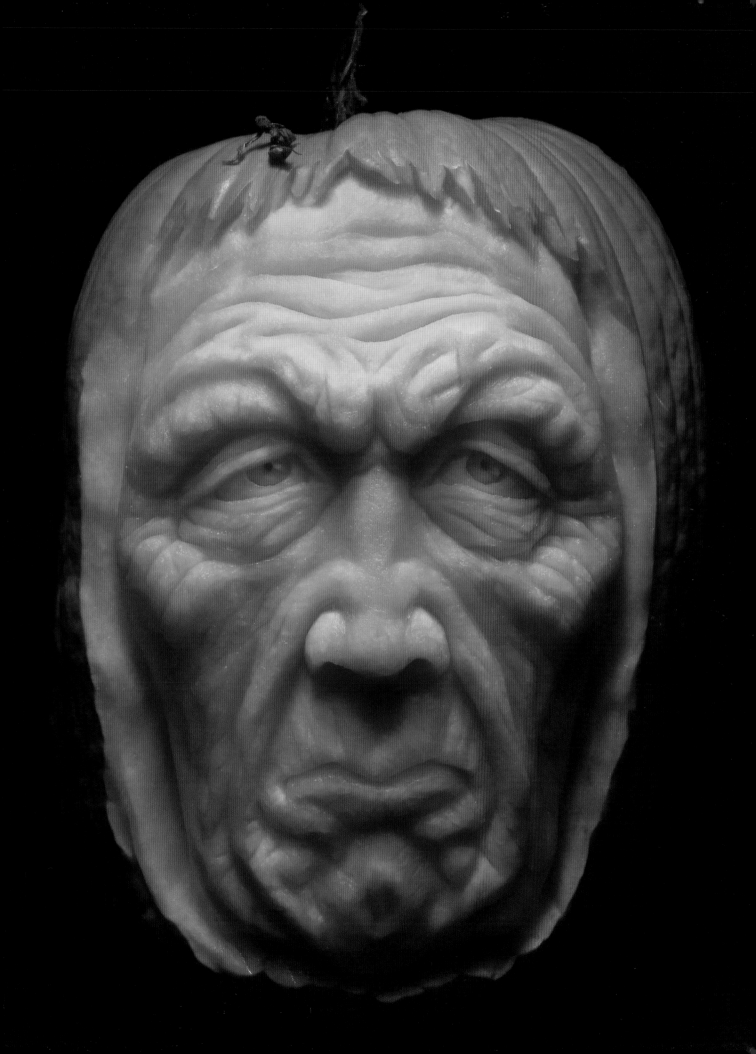

Trapped (New Moon/ White Hybrid Pumpkin)

Not So Sweet Potato

Don't Say It (New Moon/White Hybrid Pumpkin)

< Godfrey

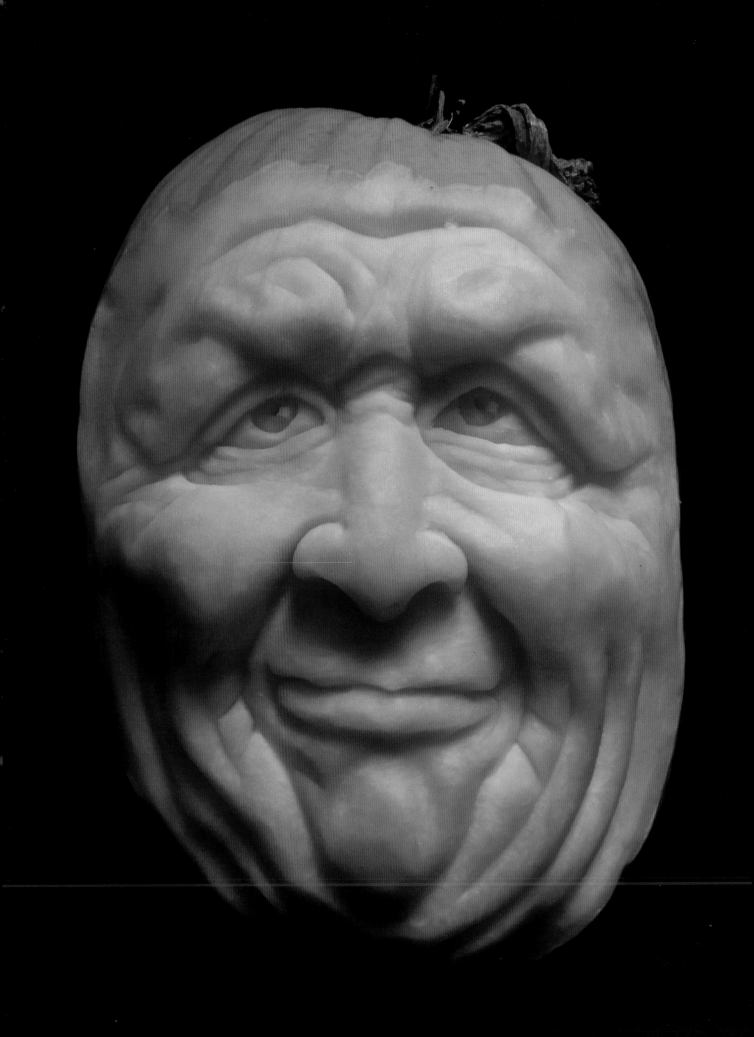

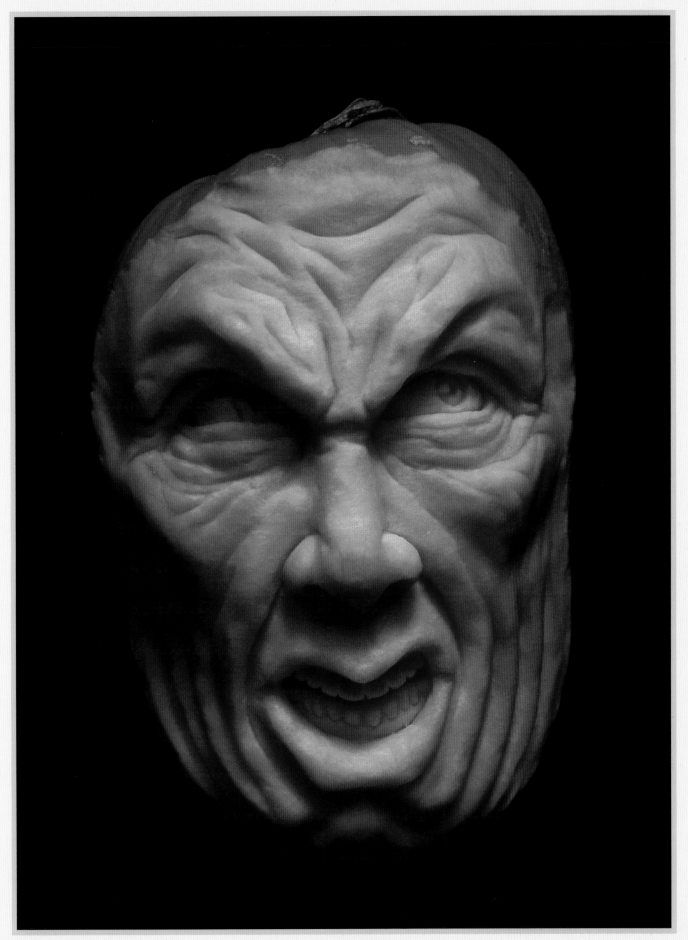

Mob Boss

Suspicious Spud

Kiss Me

Decapi-tater 1 - Napping

I Am Last

Horse Head

Do I Have To?

Shhhh

The Boxer

Pumpkin Ranger

< I Wonder

GETTING STARTED

CHOOSING A PUMPKIN

There are many varieties of pumpkins, and some are easier to carve than others. The ones with bumps that look like warts are difficult to carve; it is nearly impossible to scrape the outer skin off. Generally, the smooth-skinned varieties with shallow grooves are the best for carving.

Choose a pumpkin that feels heavy for its size; these pumpkins usually have thicker walls, which give you more room to carve. Look for a thick stem that is still green on the pumpkin. Apparently, the stem continues to nourish the pumpkin after it's harvested and will help your creation last longer. Also, press your thumb on the bottom. If it flexes or pokes through, the pumpkin is not fresh. Look for soft spots, open cuts, or mold that would indicate spoilage or damage. Finally, I prefer an oblong shape, as it lends itself to the shape of a human head. The "Howden Biggie" *Cucurbita pepo* pumpkin variety is my current favorite and is relatively common. This variety was developed by John Howden at Howden Farm in Sheffield, Mass. Every pumpkin I carved in this book is a Howden, unless noted otherwise.

If I am carving a face with a nose (which is usually the case), I look for a pumpkin with at least one protruding angle. As you can see from the top view of these pumpkins, the arrows point to the place on the pumpkin that protrudes the most. Not only do these points already lend themselves to a good place for the nose (which is usually the point on the face that protrudes the most), but they often have a thicker wall at this area. Also, don't be afraid of oddly shaped pumpkins. The shape can often lend itself to an unusual and fun end result.

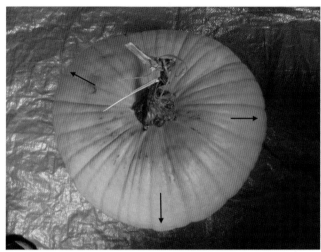

The arrows point to the places on the pumpkin that protrude the most.

TIP

Don't pick pumpkins up by the stem, which can easily break off. If the stem breaks, the pumpkin will not only lose its continued nourishment, but it also just won't look as cool.

CLEANING A PUMPKIN

Rinse the pumpkin with cold water and use a stiff plastic scrub brush to remove any dirt. Then, spray the entire pumpkin with a mild bleach solution to kill any mold and bacteria. I often wear latex or vinyl gloves when carving to prevent bacteria on my hands from prematurely molding the pumpkin, but this is not required.

CARVING TOOLS

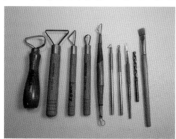 There are many types of tools you can use to carve pumpkins. Every carver has his or her favorites. There are no hard and fast rules dictating what you should use, so I suggest you explore a bit and find what works best for you. Tools range from expensive chisels, knives, and ribbon tools to basic kitchen utensils. I started with woodcarving tools because I am a woodcarver and had many on hand.

The good news is that most of these tools are not expensive. Because pumpkins are soft and relatively easy to carve, cheap woodcarving tools work just fine. They don't even have to be very sharp (although, as a habit, I try to keep all of my tools sharp and ready to go at any time). Pumpkin material won't dull them. If you are just starting out and have a few tools lying around in the basement, garage, or workshop, give them a try. You may also be surprised at the carving "tools" you'll find in the kitchen drawer—you can repurpose knives, spoons, and scoops. In the past, I have swiped a few tools from the kitchen and cut and sharpened them to the shape and degree of sharpness I prefer. Better get permission from the head chef of the house first so you're not carving pumpkins in the doghouse, though!

My pumpkin carving tools of choice are clay-sculpting ribbon tools. In general, ribbon tools are very affordable. They can be purchased at most hobby stores, although you will likely have a better selection and quality at a pottery store. If you know or have an idea what you would like to buy, shopping online can be very useful and affordable, but I think it is still more fun to go to a store and actually hold and examine tools before you buy.

I still often mix in a few woodcarving tools when I carve pumpkins. As for gouges and chisels, specific sizes are not critical. Pumpkins are more forgiving than wood.

Another very useful tool is a flexible hand-sanding pad (such as 3M or Scotch Brite). These pads smooth areas of the pumpkin for a finished look, and I often use them just before carving the final details. They can be rinsed and reused for a very long time. I also always keep a small brush around to remove shavings from the work surface.

Here is a specific list of the tools I currently use:
- Ribbon tool, large pear shaped: 1¾" (44mm) wide
- Ribbon tool, large triangle: 1¹⁵⁄₁₆" (49mm) wide
- Ribbon tool, medium triangle: 1⅜" (35mm) long
- Ribbon tool, medium teardrop: ½" (13mm) wide
- Ribbon tool, medium flat triangle: 1¼" (32mm) long
- Ribbon tool, medium dual-end: ⅜" (10mm) wide
- Ribbon tool, mini-triangle: ⁵⁄₁₆" (8mm) wide
- Ribbon tool, mini-circle: ³⁄₁₆" (5mm)
- Deep gouges: ⅛" (3mm), ¼" (6mm), ½" (13mm)
- V-tools: ⅛" (3mm), ¼" (6mm), ½" (13mm)
- Flat chisel: ½" (13mm) wide
- Scalpel with #11 blade
- Twist drill bit (size optional)

Caring For Tools

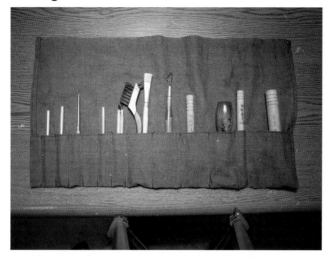

As with any tools, the better you care for your pumpkin-carving tools, the longer they will last. I keep my tools in a custom tool roll made of scrap denim cloth. Sewn pouch sections keep the tools from touching; tool edges that bang and rub together dull very quickly, so it's best to store them in a tool roll. Plus, it makes them easier to carry.

Reinforcing
This is not a necessary step, but I do it. When I purchase a new ribbon tool, I always closely examine the joint where the blade meets the handle. This is often the place where the tool is weakest and most likely to break. It's easy to get caught up in your work, apply too much pressure, and break the tool. It happens. After breaking a few myself, I have resorted to applying two-part epoxy to every new tool. It may save you from snapping a tool at a very inopportune time.

Sharpening
Sharpening isn't necessary, as pumpkin is pretty soft, but I like to keep all my tools sharp. The sharper the tool, the less pressure you have to apply, and the more control you have. I use a fine diamond stone to sharpen my ribbon tools. It doesn't take much to sharpen them; a few swipes on the sharpening stone can make a difference. Be careful with small detail tools; I've occasionally gone overboard and sharpened them so much they broke.

Cleaning
I clean all of my tools after every carving session to prolong their lives. Wet an old toothbrush or something similar with warm water to clean your tools. Be sure to dry them. Rust and corrosion begin quickly and will pit the metal, eventually dulling and then ruining the tool. When the tool is dry, spray the metal portion with WD-40. It contains anticorrosion agents and adds another layer of rust protection.

TIP

Fun Fact: The "WD" in WD-40 stands for "Water Displacement," which is just what you want on metal tool blades.

WORKSPACE

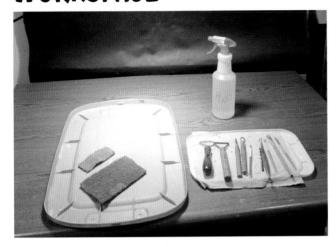

If you give pumpkin carving a go, you may be working at it for hours (or days), so you need a comfortable place to work. I won't lecture on chairs and posture, but the more comfortable you are, the longer you can carve without pain and distraction. Here are some essential elements for your workspace.

Work Surface

You need a steady table. Some pumpkins are fairly heavy and could break a lightweight table. I then put a large plastic container lid on my table and carve my pumpkins on it. The lid helps contain the mess and is easy to clean at the end of the session. I also spread my tools out on a smaller container lid. It's nice to be able to see them all and have them handy.

Lighting

Good lighting is very important for you and your project. Proper lighting prevents eyestrain and helps you see the project clearly.

Sculpture of any kind is all about lighting and shadows, so you need to position the light correctly. If you shine a light on something directly from your point of view, you see none of the contour and details. But if you shine a light on the subject from above or from the side, the shape and details are clearly visible. No matter what I'm carving, I always work with a fairly strong light directly above my subject (usually 60 watts). It helps me with depth and symmetry.

TIP

As you dive into carving, remember to take breaks regularly. Stand up, walk around, get a snack. This is good for you physically and mentally. After a break, I often come back to a pumpkin I'm carving with a new perspective and can easily see what I need to do next or what I should change.

PRESERVING THE PUMPKIN

Carved pumpkins begin to dry out as soon as you remove the outer skin. There is absolutely no consistency to the rate of decay from one pumpkin to the next; one may rot in a few days and another, carved at the same time, may last a couple of weeks. Please keep in mind that it's a pumpkin, and it will decay. Have fun and take lots of pictures with your new, temporary buddy.

I have tried many techniques and substances to preserve a carved pumpkin, from Vaseline to lacquer and about 100 things in between. I have settled on the following techniques. It seems a bit high maintenance, but it's worth it. Obviously employing all of these techniques is the best way to go, but if you can't follow all of them, just do the ones you can.

- Displaying your pumpkin: Keep it out of the sun. Display it in a relatively cool space away from direct heat and away from a breeze, such as a fan or heat vent.
- Keep the pumpkin hydrated: Add a small amount of bleach to a pump spray bottle full of water. If kids will be touching it a lot, use just water. Spray the pumpkin as often as possible. You can never spray it too much. Leaving the spray bottle nearby helps.
- Storing the pumpkin (when it's not on display): Place the pumpkin on its side, faceup if practical. Put a dripping-wet towel over the face, and put it in a plastic garbage bag. Remove as much air as possible, and close the bag with a rubber

band or twist tie. This keeps air out and moisture in. Ideally, if you have room, place it in the refrigerator; otherwise put it in the coolest place you can find. Outside will work if it's cool and won't be in the sun in the morning, but be aware that critters like pumpkins, too. Do not freeze your carved pumpkin. When it thaws, it will likely be mushy.

PHOTOGRAPHING THE PUMPKIN

There are many different ways to photograph pumpkin carvings. I prefer to photograph my pumpkins in my workshop, which can easily be transformed into a photo studio. I like to shoot all of my work (pumpkins, wood carvings, etc.) in a consistent manner. Don't let this scare you—the setup is very simple. The important thing is to just take plenty of photos of your work.

Lighting

Good lighting is key to a good photo. I use portable utility lights with aluminum reflectors and a clamp. These lights are inexpensive and can be found at any hardware store. You can experiment with wattage, but I generally use 60- to 75-watt lightbulbs.

I use anywhere from one to three lights when shooting my carvings. The most important light is usually the light directly overhead. This light both illuminates the carving and adds shadows that contribute to the dimension and depth of the photo. I will often hold it by hand as I'm shooting and move it different distances and angles to capture the best shot for that particular carving. Depending on the carving, I may place a second or third light at a different angle to slightly brighten any dark areas. I also sometimes add interest with a colored light. When you use multiple lights, be sure to not lose the detail from the overhead light.

Camera

Most modern digital cameras are easy to use and fairly inexpensive. If you're not experienced with photography, simply put the camera on auto. Don't use the zoom function; just move closer to the project.

I use a tripod and set the camera to a two-second delay. This allows me to let go of the camera and minimizes the chance of a blurry shot. Do not use a flash, as this light is usually too harsh and eliminates the details in the carving.

Backdrop

There are several options for photography backdrops. I suggest using cloth or paper. You can use a sheet, but be sure that it is clean and free of folds or wrinkles. A roll of photo background paper is a great option and can be found at photo-supply stores. I use a large roll of black, matte, seamless, heavy, professional backdrop paper. It is wrinkle-resistant, doesn't add any glare, and will last for a long time. (I've had my roll for several years.) When the paper gets marked or unusable, you just cut that portion off and unroll more.

LIGHTING THE PUMPKIN

I carved the bottom of this pumpkin, cut a hole in the top, and lit it with a 40-watt bulb so it would photograph well. However, anything from a 4- to 15-watt bulb will sufficiently light your pumpkin.

I don't usually light my pumpkins from the inside, because hollowed pumpkins generally don't last as long. If you decide to hollow your pumpkin, there are multiple ways to light it from the inside. The most common is a candle, but you can also use a battery-powered light or corded light. If you choose to use a corded light, use a low wattage bulb (4 to 15 watts). The higher the wattage, the hotter the bulb, and that heat will dry out the pumpkin faster. It usually doesn't take much to light the pumpkin.

TIP

If you decide to gut your pumpkin to install a light or candle, consider cutting the opening or "plug" in the bottom or back of the pumpkin. This keeps the top looking nice and neat.

TIP

If you are carving a silhouette-style pumpkin and intend to light it from the inside, you can remove more of the interior flesh. The thinner the pumpkin, the brighter the inside light will appear as it shines through the shallow surface cuts.

CARVING GOURDS, SQUASH, AND SWEET POTATOES

Pumpkins are clearly the most popular for carving in the fall (Halloween). However, there are many other wonderful edible things that you can carve any time of year. Explore the produce section of the grocery store and get to know different varieties. You'll see fruits and veggies in a whole new way.

Carving Gourds and Squash
Before you carve a gourd or squash, make sure to clean it using the process for cleaning a pumpkin (see page 27). Again, be careful not to break off the stem, if there is one.

Some winter gourds have a very hard shell that can only be removed with a chisel and a mallet. This was the case with Gele, a yellow autumn wings gourd (see page 34). I chiseled away the thin shell where I wanted to carve, and once I got through, the flesh was thick and easy to carve.

Some gourds and squash have thicker flesh walls, which makes them a real treat to carve. The thicker the walls, the more depth you can carve into the face. One such squash is the butternut squash, which can be found easily in many regions and is a treat to carve. The flesh is generally a good carving density and thick, giving you lots of area for depth.

On the other hand, I've found that the common spaghetti squash is not a good choice for carving. This squash gets its name from its spaghetti-like flesh, which is very stringy and doesn't hold detail.

Carving Sweet Potatoes, or "Decapi-Taters"
Sweet potatoes are one of my favorite vegetables to carve. They are a bit denser than pumpkins but carve well. They also have great color—the orange flesh shows more detail than a white potato, and it just looks cool. Sweet potatoes are usually

available any time of the year in many locations and are inexpensive. This makes them great for experimenting!

I have had to explain myself more than once in the produce aisle at the grocery store. I would go through a hundred sweet potatoes examining each one as carefully as if I were picking out a car. People would just stare. Employees would inevitably come over and ask if they could help me with anything. Sometimes I would explain myself and produce a few photos to clear things up.

Carving Your Tater

Clean a sweet potato using the process for cleaning a pumpkin. I'm a little gentler when cleaning sweet potatoes because I like the look of the intact skin on the uncarved areas. I also use the same tools to carve potatoes as I do pumpkins. Because the flesh of a potato is harder than that of a pumpkin, don't be overly aggressive with deep cuts because you can break your tools. (This statement comes from experience.) Take your time and make several shallow cuts instead of deep ones. This gives you control over your tools and your progress, and will save your tools in the long run.

As with pumpkins, I start by removing the skin in the area to be carved. Then, you can transfer a pattern to the potato or use a marker or a finishing nail to sketch a few of the basic features. Once I have established

the basic facial features, I carve the brow line and under the nose. Then, it's just a matter of carving everything away from the area that's supposed to protrude the most, like the nose. Another great thing about potatoes is they don't have a hollow core like a pumpkin. You can carve as deeply as you like.

Preserving Your Tater

The first and most important way to preserve your creation is to take photos. Like your pumpkin creations, take the best photos you can so you can enjoy your work long after they're gone (See Photographing the Pumpkin on page 30). Beyond that, there are other options. Unlike pumpkins, sweet potatoes can be preserved fairly easily.

- Dry the potato. Keep the potato in a dry environment. The potato will keep its general shape and shrivel up, which creates lots of great wrinkles. To avoid mold, add a small amount of bleach to a pump spray bottle full of water. Give the tater a good spray, and let it sit. You may need to spray it a couple of times, but that will prevent the potato from getting moldy. You'll know the potato is completely dried when it resembles and feels like wood. Dried sweet potatoes are lightweight and hard. I still have the first one I carved, a few years ago, sitting in my studio and it hasn't changed. It's a petrified spud.

- Preserve the potato. Fill a jar with vinegar or isopropyl or ethyl alcohol, and plop the potato in. If preserving something in vinegar seems familiar, it is—this is how you pickle food. But you won't be eating your potato, so you don't need all the spices and complications of that process. Just drop your spud in a jar and pour in the vinegar. If you use alcohol, don't eat your potato. If this is a concern, use vinegar. If you preserve your tater with alcohol or vinegar, it won't shrivel up and will remain as you carved it for a very long time. I have a couple in jars from two years ago and they still look great. If the alcohol or vinegar gets cloudy, pour it out and replace it.

HOW DECAPI-TATERS GOT THEIR NAME

I have to give credit where credit is due. The name "Decapi-tater" did not originate in my warped brain, but came from the next best thing. Humor me while I reveal the true genius behind this absolutely perfect name.

When I first sat down to attempt to carve sweet potatoes, I wasn't thinking of what I could call them. Heck, I had no idea how they would carve or how they would turn out, let alone what to call them. Because I'd been carving other materials like wood for a few years at this point, I dove in to get a feel for the material and to see how the tools worked with it. The first few turned out okay and, like anything else, they got better fairly quickly with practice. Then, at one point, I nailed it. I love that feeling when something comes together after a bit of practice.

That's when I thought that there has to be a clever name for these things. So I kept carving, experimenting, and trying to think of that perfect name for about a week. Nothing. I had nothing. At this point, I grudgingly admitted that I might need to ask for ideas from someone else. Oh, the shame! I mean, I'm supposed to be the all-creative artist here, right? I took one of my wicked sweet potato creations to my young teenage son's room and knocked on the door.

"Yeah?"

"I need your help with something. Can I ask you a question?"

"Yeah." (He's a teenage boy. You don't often get much more than that).

I entered his room, where he sat at his desk working at three computer monitors,

hacking into satellites or working for the National Security Agency or something. He didn't even turn around.

"Hey buddy, I've been trying to come up with a clever name for my sweet potato carvings for a week and I got nothin'. Can you help me out here?"

He nonchalantly turned around and looked at what I was holding. Didn't touch it—just barely gave it a glance and turned back to his binary sorcery. I waited patiently, not sure if he was aware that I was still in the room.

After about 10 seconds, he said in a low and even tone, "Decapi-taters."

I processed what he just said and it started to dawn on me. Then, still working on whatever world problems he was solving (or creating), he said, "Get it, Dad? It's a head and a potato. You know, like a tater?"

I was stunned. I'm sure I had a ridiculous, dumbfounded expression on my face.

He asked if I needed anything else, and I pulled myself together and mumbled something incoherent about how brilliant that is.

"Nope, that's it. Great job, son. Thanks. Carry on," I said.

I don't think a marketing company with thousands of my dollars could have come up with anything even close to this good. I'd been trying to come up with a name for weeks, and it took a distracted teenage boy 10 seconds. But at least it was my distracted teenage boy. Never hurts to ask for a little help every now and then, huh?

PROJECTS

BEGINNER STEP-BY-STEP: GELE

Carving an autumn wings gourd is similar to carving any soft material—once you get past the outer shell. This is where it differs from carving pumpkins or sweet potatoes. The shell is thin but hard, like plastic, and requires a bit more than just a scraper. Otherwise, carving this gourd is a real treat. The walls are thick, and the flesh is perfect for carving and holding detail. Other than removing the outer shell, I carved the entire gourd with clay-sculpting ribbon tools.

MATERIALS & TOOLS

Materials:
- Gourd
- Bleach
- Latex gloves
- Spray bottle of water
- Sanding pad, such as 3M: medium grit

Tools:
- ¾" (19mm) #7 gouge (gently curved gouge)
- Mallet
- Ribbon tool, large triangle: 1¹⁵⁄₁₆" (49mm) wide
- Ribbon tool, medium dual-end: ⅜" (10mm) wide
- Ribbon tool, mini-triangle: ⁵⁄₁₆" (8mm) wide
- Scalpel with #11 blade
- Twist drill bit

GETTING STARTED

Clean the gourd before you begin to carve. Rinse the gourd with cold water and use a stiff plastic scrub brush to remove any dirt. Then, spray the entire gourd with a mild bleach solution to kill any mold and bacteria.

I suggest placing a light directly above your work area; this will cast a strong shadow and will help with symmetry and depth.

 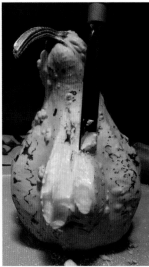

1 **Remove the shell.** Use a ¾" (19mm) #7 gouge, which has a gentle curve, and a mallet to remove the shell from the area to be carved. I don't remove a large area of the shell; I actually prefer to keep as much shell as possible because it adds interest when the carving is finished. You can always remove more as you're carving if necessary.

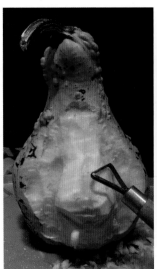 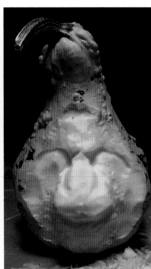

2 **Establish the brow line and nose.** Smooth the flesh of the gourd with a 1¹⁵⁄₁₆" (49mm) large triangle ribbon tool. Then, use a ⅜" (10mm) medium dual-end ribbon tool to make shallow cuts where the brow line and nose will be.

TIP

The Design
If you want to draw the face, use a dry-erase marker. If you don't like the face, you can erase it and start over. An orange marker will be visible enough and will be easy to erase.

3 **Rough out the face.** Use the ⅜" (10mm) medium dual-end ribbon tool to carve away the material surrounding the tip of the nose. Rough out the size and shape of the nose, form eye sockets, and begin the barrel of the mouth. If necessary, remove more of the outer shell to expose more flesh. Smooth the surface with a sanding pad.

Beginner: Adding the Details

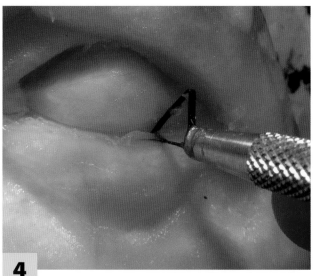

4 **Carve the eyes and eyelids.** Using the ⁵⁄₁₆" (8mm)-wide mini-triangle ribbon tool, cut the eyelids and round the eyeballs. Make V-shaped cuts for sags and wrinkles under and around the eyes, forehead, and mouth.

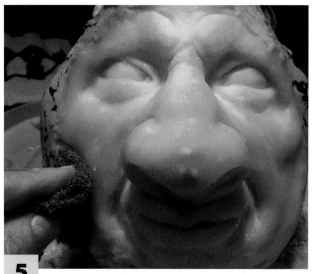

5 **Carve the nostrils and lips.** Carve around the sides of the nose with the ⁵⁄₁₆" (8mm)-wide mini-triangle ribbon tool. Then, use the ⅜" (10mm) medium dual-end ribbon tool to carve the nostrils. Determine the shapes of the lips and carve them with the ⁵⁄₁₆" (8mm)-wide mini-triangle ribbon tool. This will begin to create expression. Smooth the surface with the medium-grit sanding pad.

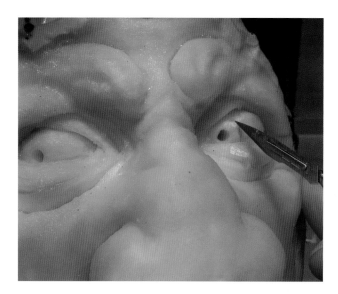

6 Carve the pupils and irises. Decide where the gourd is looking and bore a clean hole for each pupil. I hold a twist drill bit between my thumb and index finger, and drill the hole with a quick twist of my wrist. Then, use a scalpel with a #11 blade to cut around the irises; aim to maintain an equal distance from the pupils. After you've carved the outer circles, make V-shaped cuts to deepen each iris. If you want to add a "gleam" to the eyes, leave a rectangle in the same place in each eye.

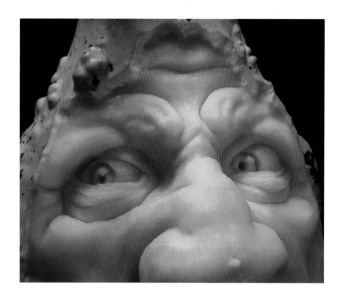

7 Complete the carving. Make V-shaped cuts for sags and wrinkles under and around the eyes, forehead, and mouth smile lines. Finish with another smoothing with the sanding pad, being careful not to remove the carved details.

TIP

Focus the Eyes

To focus both eyes in the same direction, make a dot with a marker or create a small, shallow hole in one eye and match its place on the other eye. Be sure it is shallow enough that if it's not correct, you can carve it away without removing much material.

BEGINNER PATTERN: GELE
Autumn Wings Gourd

ADVANCED STEP-BY-STEP: UNCLE GOURDY

You may feel confused by this pumpkin's name—Uncle Gourdy? It's not a gourd, it's a pumpkin. But gourds and pumpkins are actually the same thing—they're both squash! Gourds are inedible squash, and pumpkins are edible, round squash.

MATERIALS & TOOLS

Materials:
- Pumpkin
- Bleach
- Latex gloves
- Spray bottle of water
- Sanding pad, such as 3M: medium grit

Tools:
- Ribbon tool, large triangle: 1¹⁵⁄₁₆" (49mm) wide
- Deep gouges: ⅛" (3mm), ¼" (6mm), ½" (13mm)
- V-tools: ⅛" (3mm), ¼" (6mm), ½" (13mm)
- Flat chisel: ½" (13mm) wide
- Scalpel with #11 blade
- Twist drill bit

GETTING STARTED

Rinse the pumpkin with cold water and use a stiff plastic scrub brush to remove any dirt. Then, spray the entire pumpkin with a mild bleach solution to kill any mold and bacteria. I sometimes wear latex or vinyl gloves when carving to prevent bacteria on my hands from prematurely molding the pumpkin.

As with any carving, a light directly above your work area that casts a strong shadow will help with symmetry and depth.

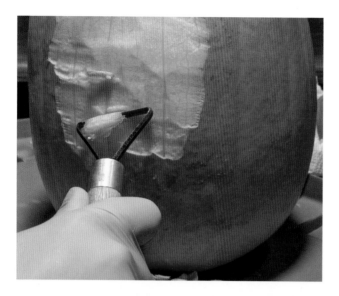

1 **Remove the skin.** Use a peeler to remove the outer orange skin in the area to be carved; I use a 1¹⁵⁄₁₆" (49mm) large triangle ribbon tool. Try not to take too much of the pumpkin meat in the process. A pumpkin begins to dry as soon as the skin is removed, so spray it with water while you carve to keep it hydrated and pliable.

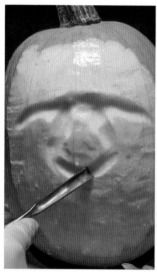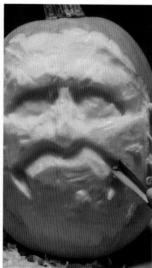

2 **Establish the main features.** Using a ½" (13mm) gouge, make shallow cuts where the brow line and nose will be. Then, carve the eye sockets and begin the barrel of the mouth with a ½" (13mm) V-tool.

3 **Create some depth.** Switch back and forth between the ½" (13mm) gouge and the ½" (13mm) V-tool as you work to create depth and shadow in the carving. Round the eye sockets and begin to separate the brows from the forehead. Establish the cheeks and carve them down to separate them from the nose. Deepen the mouth barrel into the sides, and outline the nose. The tip of the nose protrudes more than any other area, so carve everything else deeper.

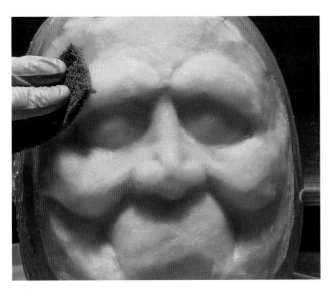

4 **Smooth the surface.** After you've carved most of the main features, sand and smooth the surface with a medium-grit sanding pad. This makes it easier to see where you need to adjust the main features before adding details.

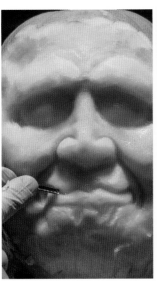
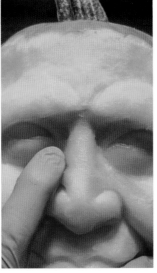

5 **Rough in the mouth.** This is where you start to create expression in the carving. Redraw the mouth if necessary. Use a ⅛" (3mm) V-tool to carve the space between the lips to separate the top and bottom lips. Then, use a ½" (13mm) gouge to carve under the bottom lip. It is usually not necessary to carve above the top lip because it is less pronounced than the bottom one.

TIP

Determining the Thickness of an Area

Gently pressing on an area with your finger will give you a good idea how much pumpkin flesh remains. If it is still quite solid, that means you have more flesh to remove, if desired.

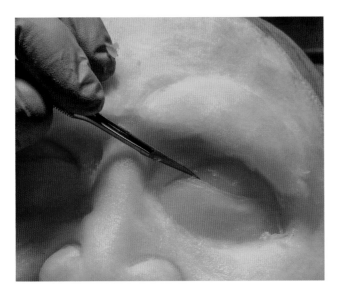

6 **Define the eyes.** Use a scalpel with a #11 blade to make V-shaped cuts for the upper and lower eyelids. Then, round the eyeballs by carving small portions away from the edges. The deepest part of the carving is the inner corner of the eye (closest to the bridge of the nose), so I try to make this part as deep as possible without carving through the pumpkin wall (see Tip).

7 Add the wrinkles. This is where the pumpkin really begins to develop character. Again switching back and forth between various V-tools and gouges, add lines and wrinkles of varying depths to the outsides of the eyes, lower eyelids, forehead, and smile lines in the cheeks.

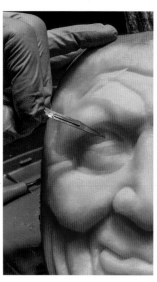 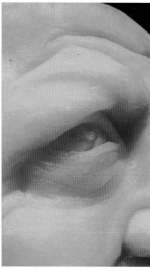

8 Carve the pupils and irises. Use a twist drill bit to bore holes for the pupils. Once the pupils are done, use a scalpel to make V-cuts for the irises; try to maintain an equal distance from the pupil. If you would like a "gleam" in the eyes, leave a square high spot in the iris and cut deeper around it. Make this high spot in the same place on both eyes.

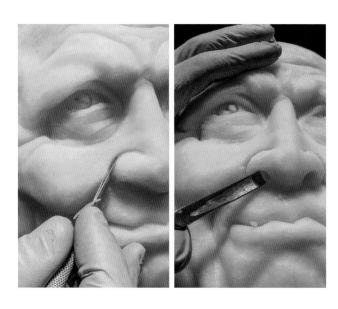

9 **Sharpen and define the details.** Use the scalpel to make V cuts anywhere there is a crevice, such as the eye and forehead wrinkles, between the lips, and outside the nostrils. This makes the details look crisp and clean. Carve the nostrils last because they are delicate. Use a small gouge or a drill bit held between your thumb and finger to bore the nostril holes.

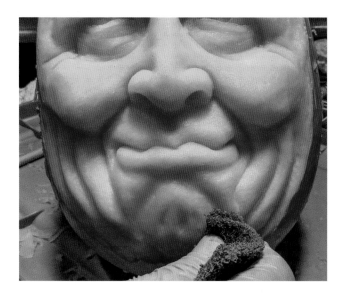

10 **Smooth the face again.** Use the medium-grit sanding pad to give the face a soft and finished look. Faces don't have any sharp edges or flat planes, so round everything.

TECHNIQUES

CARVING TEETH

There are so many different kinds of teeth you can give your pumpkin—scary fangs, rotten nubs, crooked teeth, or straight pearly whites an orthodontist would envy. This section will cover the basics to get you started. When you feel comfortable, start experimenting! Carve different kinds of teeth and see how they add to each carving.

MATERIALS & TOOLS

Materials:
· Pumpkin

Tools:
· Finishing nail
· Ribbon tool, mini-triangle: ⁵⁄₁₆" (8mm) wide
· Ribbon tool, mini-circle: ³⁄₁₆" (5mm)
· Scalpel with #11 blade

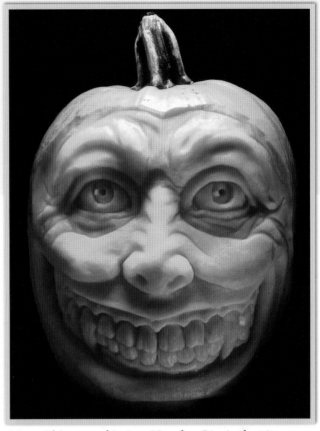

Note: This pumpkin is a Howden Biggie, but it was picked and carved before it was fully ripened. This is why some of the skin and flesh have a greenish tint.

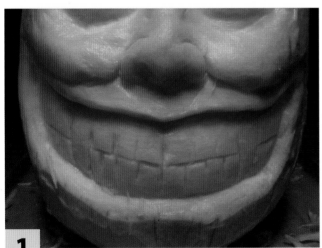

1 **Outline the teeth.** After you've carved the mouth and decided where the teeth will be, use a finishing nail or other pointy object to lightly mark the location of each tooth.

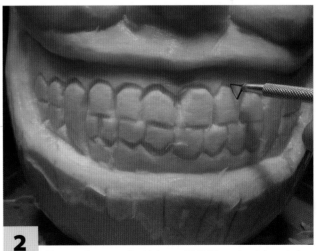

2 **Carve the teeth.** Using a ⁵⁄₁₆" (8mm)-wide mini-triangle ribbon tool, carve around each tooth. Look at photos to see different shapes of teeth and how the gums curve as they meet each tooth. Don't focus on the details of each individual tooth; instead focus on carving each tooth to the same degree. This will make for a more overall uniform end result.

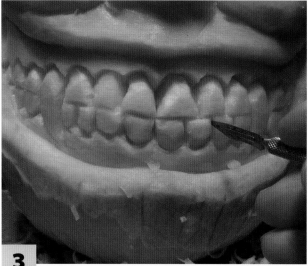

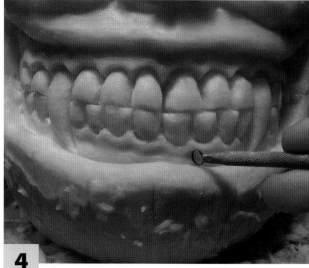

3 **Add the details.** Use a scalpel with a #11 blade or a razor knife to cut in deeper between each tooth and around the gums. Again, work your way through all of them to the same degree and depth. After carving all the teeth, use a small piece of a sanding pad to smooth and slightly round each tooth.

4 **Shape the gums.** As you can see in the mirror or in photos, the gums protrude slightly between each tooth. They also bulge a bit where the unseen portion of the tooth goes into and under the gums. Use the ³⁄₁₆" (5mm) mini-circle ribbon tool to lightly carve the gum area just above or below each tooth where it meets the gums. This detail gives the teeth a more realistic look.

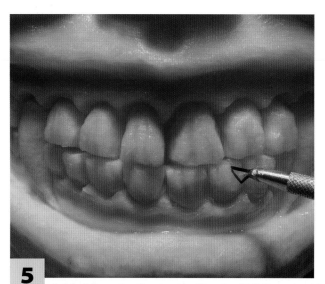

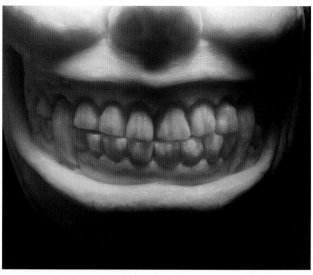

5 **Add ridges to the teeth.** Use the ⁵⁄₁₆" (8mm)-wide mini-triangle ribbon tool to very lightly carve ridges into each tooth. The surfaces of teeth are generally not perfectly smooth and flat. Light vertical ridges give them an accented, realistic look.

TOOTHY GRIN

Howden Biggie

CARVING EYES

The eyes are the most important feature of your pumpkin carving. Eyes portray expression and mood. For example, when you carve a smiling mouth, it just looks like a smile. But when you add the eyes, you determine whether the smile is happy or evil, sly or sincere, conniving or angelic.

However, eyes can also be the most challenging feature to carve. But don't worry—they're also my favorite feature to carve. Here's a tutorial to show you how to carve eyes. I used a New Moon/White Hybrid pumpkin to carve this face.

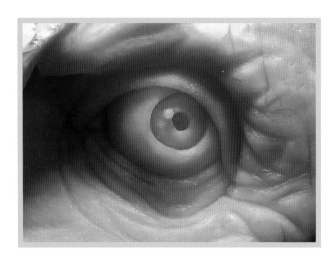

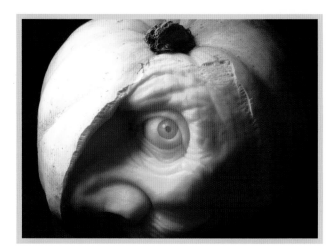

MATERIALS & TOOLS

Materials:
· Pumpkin
· Sanding pad, such as 3M: medium grit

Tools:
· Finishing nail
· Ribbon tool, medium dual-end: ⅜" (10mm) wide
· Ribbon tool, mini-triangle: ⁵⁄₁₆" (8mm) wide
· Scalpel with #11 blade
· Twist drill bit

1 **Establish the brow line.** Use a ⅜" (10mm) medium dual-end ribbon tool to carve the brow line. The brow line helps shape the eyes. The brow line pictured here is relatively neutral, because I chose to show only one eye. You can lower the brow in the center to make a scowl or raise the brow in the center and slope it toward the outer corner of each eye to create a worried expression.

2 **Carve the eye socket.** Establish the general shape of the eye in the socket with the ⅜" (10mm) medium dual-end ribbon tool. Remember, the eye is a sphere, so imagine a sphere just below the surface of the skin. This can be a fairly large area because it will consist of both the eyeball and upper and lower eyelids. Smooth the area with a sanding pad.

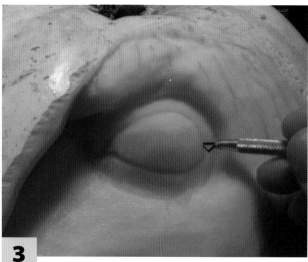

3 **Carve the eye and the eyelids.** Use a ⁵⁄₁₆" (8mm)-wide mini-triangle ribbon tool to make V-shaped cuts to separate the eyeball from the upper and lower eyelids. Don't forget to carve the caruncle (the triangular bump on the inner corner of the eye).

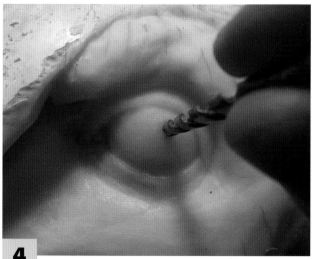

4 **Carve the pupil.** Determine where you want the pumpkin to look, and bore a hole for the pupil by twisting a drill bit between your fingers. This makes a nice clean hole. The deeper you go, the darker the pupil will look.

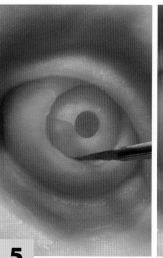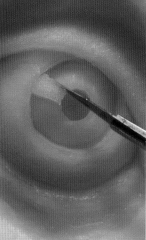

5 **Carve the iris.** Use a scalpel with a #11 blade to cut the iris; try to maintain an equal distance from the pupil. Then, make V-shaped cuts to deepen the iris, making sure to leave a raised rectangle between the pupil and iris to create a "gleam" in the eye.

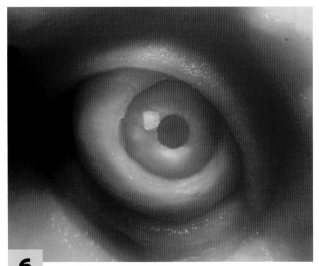 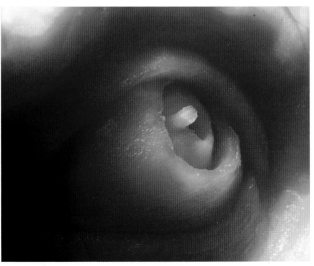

6 **Define the gleam.** Use the scalpel to carefully carve away the section of the gleam that connects the gleam to the outer edge of the iris, leaving the section that is closest to the pupil. Round the edges of the gleam. Notice in the side view close-up how the gleam extends above the iris. This is also a good time to make V-cuts around and under the eyelids to give them more definition.

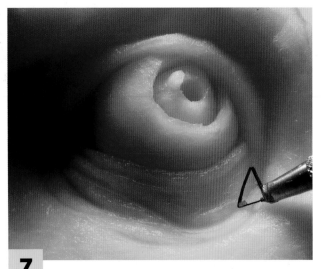 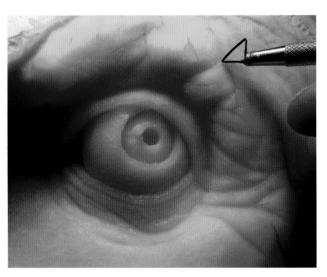

7 **Carve the lower eyelid.** Use the ⁵⁄₁₆" (8mm)-wide mini-triangle ribbon tool to carve wrinkles in the lower lid and the laugh lines around the eye and brow. Tuck the lower eyelid under the upper eyelid on the outer corner of the eye. This makes the eye look more realistic.

AN EYE ON THE SITUATION
New Moon/White Hybrid Pumpkin

PATTERNS

COUNT GOURDULA
Jarrahdale Pumpkin

KEEPIN' AN EYE ON YOU

Howden Biggie

ZIPPERHEAD

Howden Biggie

THE WITCH
Howden Biggie

Note: Carve the flower in the bottom of the pumpkin, centering the design around the blossom mark.

FLOWER
Howden Biggie

SPUD ZOMBIE
Sweet Potato

BAD DAY

Howden Biggie & Mini Pumpkin

STEM NOSE

Howden Biggie

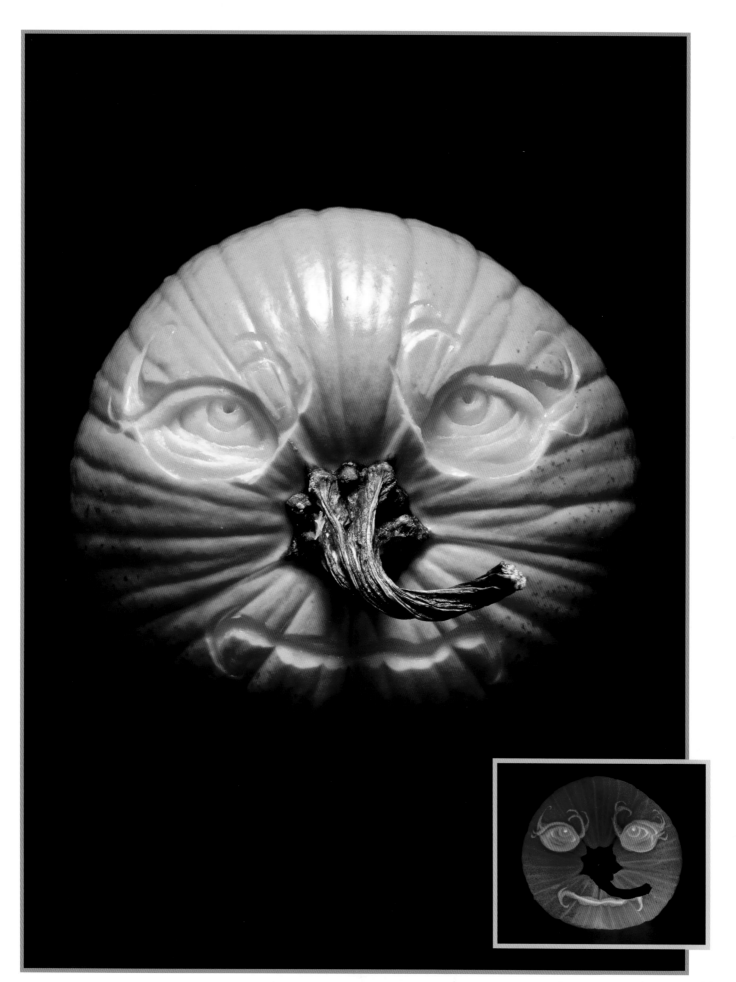

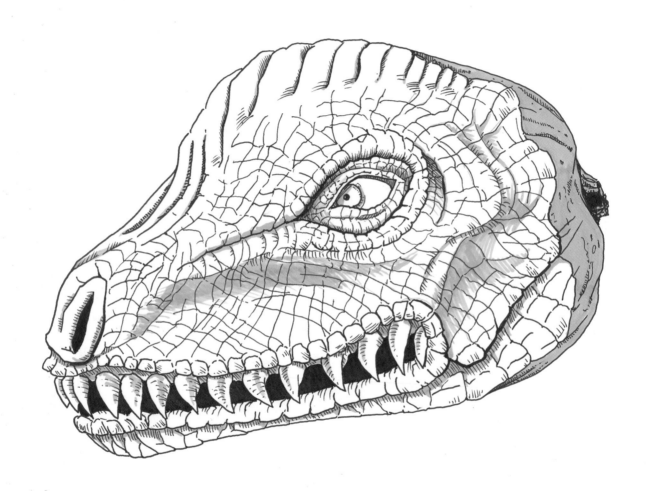

P-REX

Howden Biggie

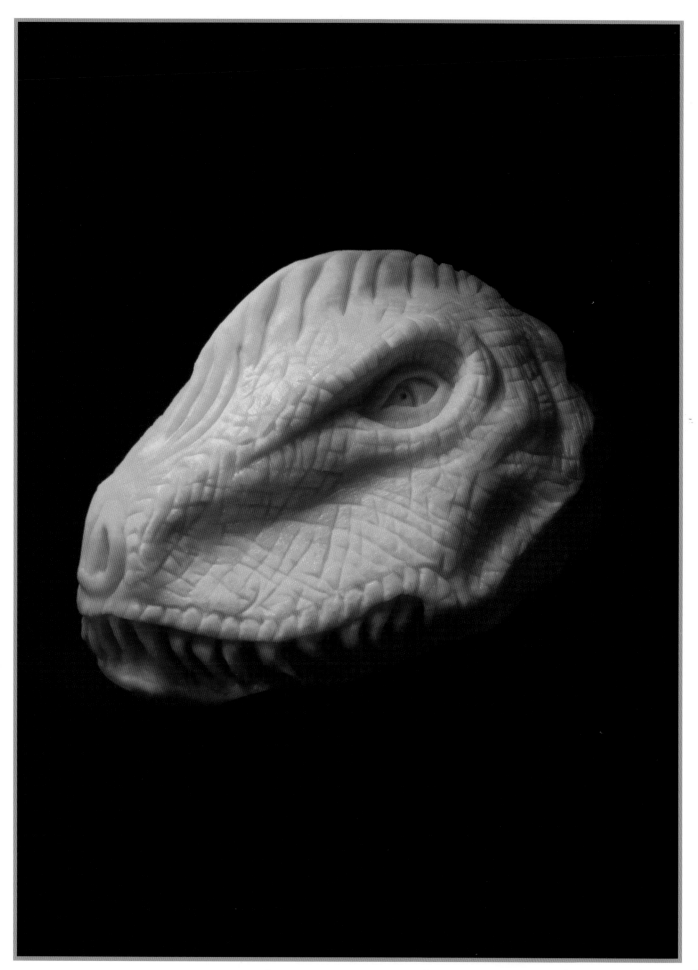

ELFIS SPUDLY

Sweet Potato

APE MONSTER
Howden Biggie

HOLD YOUR BREATH
Sweet Potato

WORRIED

Howden Biggie

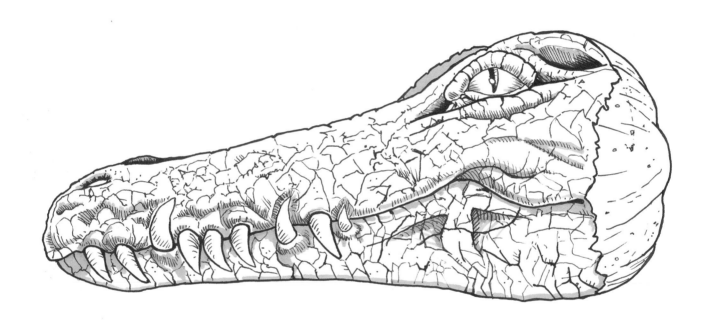

BUTTERNUT CROC

Butternut Squash

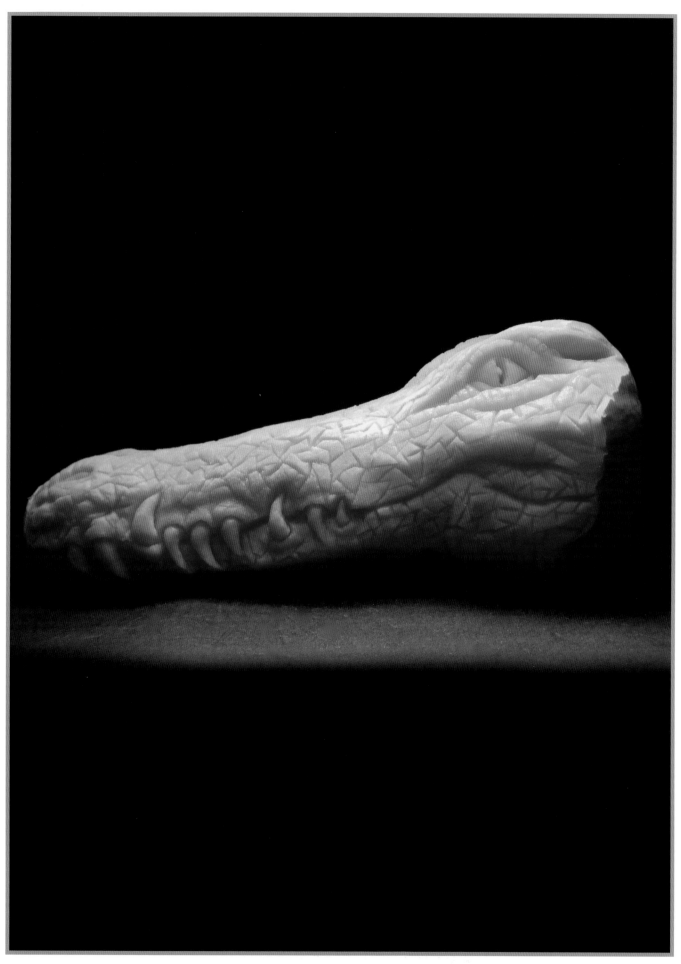

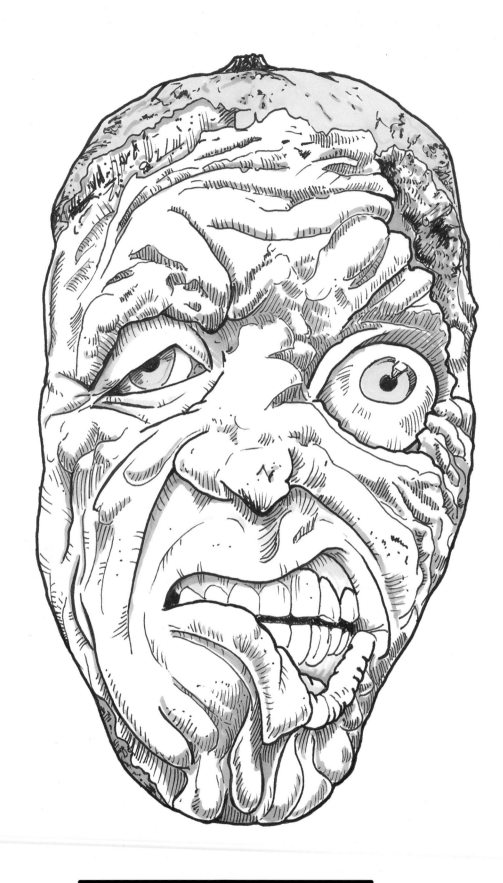

SWEET POTACALYPSE

Sweet Potato

MOUNTAIN MAN

Howden Biggie

HALF SKULL

New Moon/White Hybrid

JACK

Howden Biggie

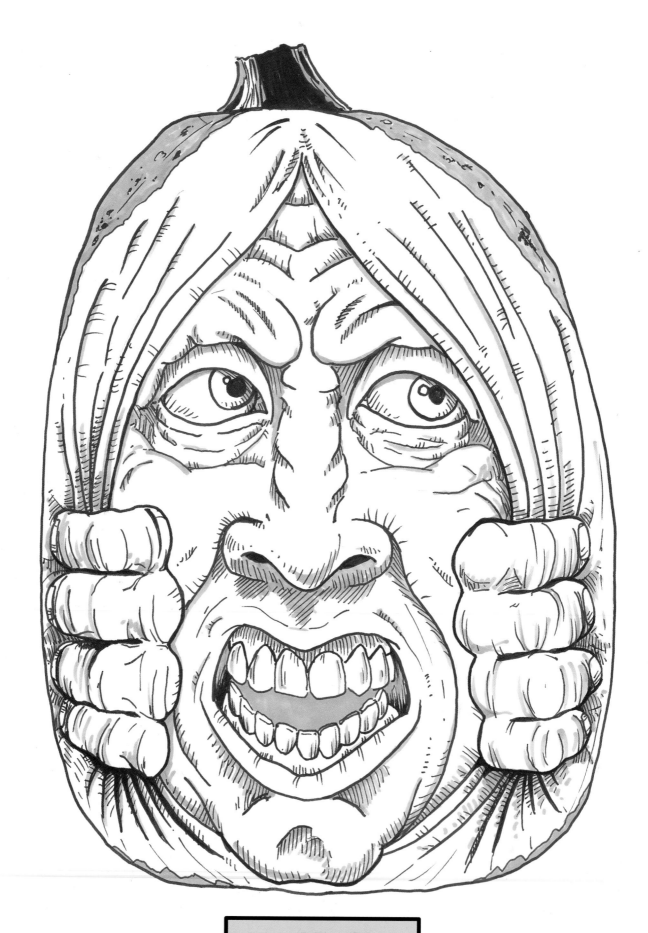

LET ME OUT

Howden Biggie

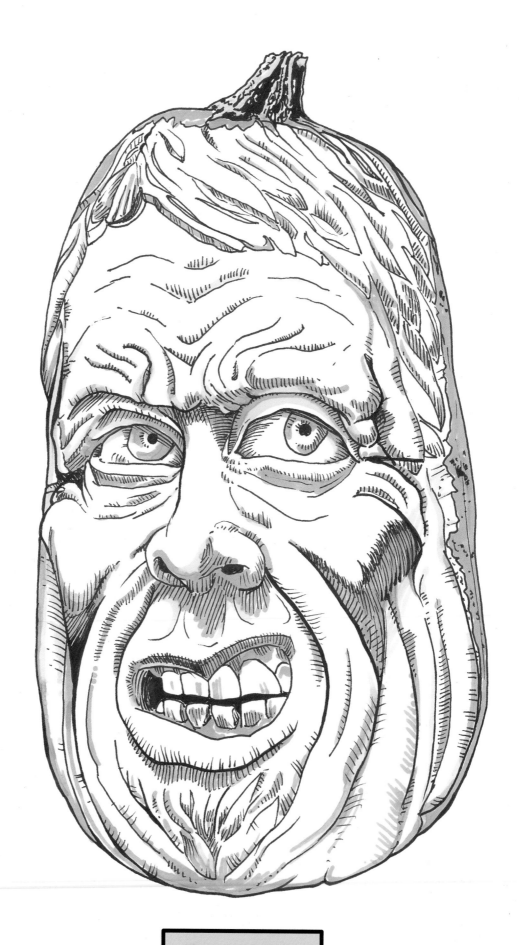

GOURDON

Howden Biggie

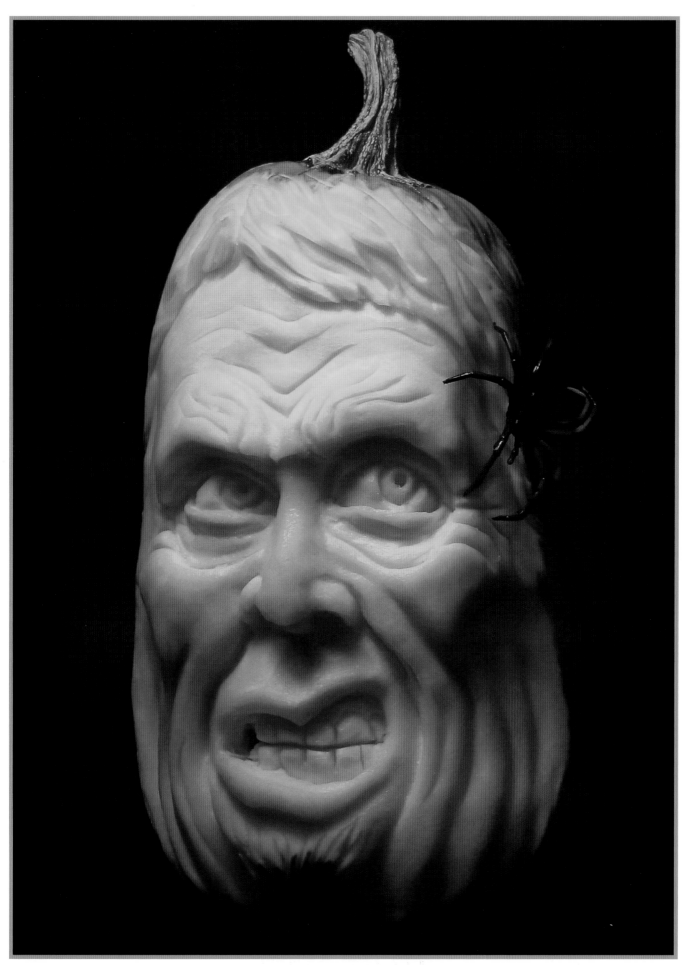

ACKNOWLEDGMENTS

There are many people who helped make my venture into the world of art not only possible but successful.

First, I have to thank the friends who kindly tolerated my excitement and constant babble about my ideas and current projects. They very patiently listened to the same stories over and over as I told them to new acquaintances inquiring about my work. My brave friends were also subjected to viewing photos of all of my "masterpieces" and said kind things. There are too many of you to mention by name, so thank you. You know who you are.

Then, there are those who actually had a hand in teaching and guiding me through a world of business and art—a world I had no idea how to navigate. A few of these people took me under their wings and never hesitated to answer my questions. Thank you also to those who have helped my work and me get noticed in the media. All of these people are professional, successful, and very talented. I am proud to also call them my friends.
A few of those generous people are:

- Lisa Jennings, LisaJenningsArt.com. Her accessibility, encouragement, and willingness to share her wealth of knowledge were beyond generous.
- Anton Weiss, professional artist. He is a truly wise and inspirational individual who didn't hesitate to share his insight and knowledge.
- Sharon and Randy Ingram of Mud Puddle Pottery, Harpethartcenter.com. They had faith in my potential and gave me a place to display my work from the beginning.
- Rick Malkin, professional photographer. He gave me enough pointers to make my work look good and consistent. He's also a pretty funny guy.
- Terry Bulger, feature reporter, author, and freelance television journalist. Terry was the first person to bring me and my work to television, first on his Nashville NBC affiliate newscast feature and then on a PBS featured segment. He is a talented, kind, and generous man who brings a positive perspective to the world.
- And yes, the staff at Fox Chapel Publishing. They had the confidence in me to not only offer the opportunity to be a contributor to *Woodcarving Illustrated* magazine but also to do this book. They are true professionals and have been a pleasure to work with.

Penny, thank you for giving me the opportunity to discover myself as an artist.

I thank my dad, who died six years before I even knew I had any artistic ability. All of my life, he encouraged me to try things and discover the world (in a mental, not a geographical sense). He instilled that sense of wonder in me when I was very young. He also advised me to go through life in such a way that I would never look back when my time is up and say to myself, "I wish I would have tried that ... What if?" I took that to heart and have pretty much lived my life that way. (I'm certain he'd be grinning ear-to-ear right now.) Thanks, Dad.

And thank you to Mom, who has always been very supportive and full of love. She had three sons, and I think we all turned out pretty well. She also has quite a sense of humor, which no doubt helps in every situation, especially with three sons. My two brothers, Louis and Michael, have always been there for me, even though they lived far away. We are three very different people, but we love one another, and I've always known they have my back.

I feel I have been lucky so far because nearly everyone I've encountered in this pursuit has been wonderful.

Thank you all for your support, inspiration, patience, and tolerance.

Lundy

Lundy

INDEX

Note: Page numbers in *italics* indicate patterns and projects.